THE LAW OF FALLING BODIES

The Law
of Falling Bodies

· · ·   · ·   · ·   · · ·

POEMS BY
ELTON GLASER

The University of Arkansas Press
Fayetteville • 2013

ISBN-10: 1-55728-996-4
ISBN-13: 978-1-55728-996-4

17 16 15 14 13   5 4 3 2 1

Designed by Liz Lester

⊖ The paper used in this publication meets the minimum requirements
of the American National Standard for Permanence of Paper for
Printed Library Materials Z39.48-1984.

LIBRARY OF CONGRESS CATALOGING-IN-PUBLICATION DATA

Glaser, Elton.
⎾Poems. Selections⏌
The law of falling bodies : poems / by Elton Glaser.
    pages   cm
Poems.
ISBN-13: 978-1-55728-996-4 (paper : alk. paper)
ISBN-10: 1-55728-996-4 (paper : alk. paper)
I. Title.
PS3557.L314L39   2013
811'.6—dc23

                    2012039716

for Helen, *forever*

ACKNOWLEDGMENTS

I gratefully acknowledge the magazines in which these poems were first published, some in a slightly different form. *Alligator Juniper:* "Drinking Alone on a Spring Day." *Arroyo Literary Review:* "Exit Strategy." *Chest:* "Ceremony." *Cimarron Review:* "Down on the Farm" (now "Girl down on the Farm"). *Dogwood:* "At the Casino with Justice," "Downwind from the Uplift." *Field:* "Bottoming Out," "Gifts out of Dirty Weather," "Where the Mississippi Begins." *Main Street Rag:* "It Ain't the Heat, It's the Stupidity." *New Ohio Review:* "In the Season of Early Dark." *OnEarth:* "During the Deluge," "Incantations of April." *River Styx:* "Thanksgiving in New Orleans, 2005." *Shenandoah:* "Church of the Downtown Redeemer and Twiceborn Saints," "May Rain," "Squall Lines." *Slant:* "After the Harvest, before the Snow." *The Southern Poetry Review:* "Do the Do." "Church of the Downtown Redeemer and Twiceborn Saints" was reprinted in *Joyful Noise: An Anthology of American Spiritual Poetry*, ed. Robert Strong (Pittsburgh, PA: Autumn House Press, 2007). "Do the Do" was reprinted in *Pushcart Prize XXXVII: Best of the Small Presses*, ed. Bill Henderson, with Bob Hicok and Maxine Kumin (New York: W. W. Norton, 2013).

Some of these poems were given guidance by the poetry workshop in Akron to which I belong. And special thanks to William Greenway and Lynn Powell, for their encouragement and advice.

CONTENTS

III.

IV.

I.

The earth is a twitchy system.
—Robert Socolow

. . .

And Nature gave a second groan.
—John Milton

Where the Mississippi Begins

In a trickle of northern water, clear and cold,
Knuckling over the low stones, who could tell
It would spread out, nosing
Those slow miles of scrub and rushes,
Fattening on its own lazy swell,
Then muscle its way down the Midwest, past ports
And pine bogs and towns with twelve churches and one whore,
River on a mission, from flood rise to mud bottom,
Sliding in a long swoon around New Orleans, picking up
Barges and broken logs and shrimp boats bound for the Gulf,
A dirty splurge reeling in fish spawn and essence of oil,
Until all those drops carried from its high pure source
Marry the brown waters warming toward Mexico—
And what wouldn't I give
To put my mouth to its mouth, and taste again
That strange flow, that blur pouring down the motherland,
Half junk, half jubilee?

Squall Lines

The long-limbed roses
Lash the rain like buggy whips
Driving the day home. And that's as it should be,

After a morning that went from bed to bad,
Noon of fidgets and snarls,
Evening so flimsy it falls apart

At the crunch of thunder,
Lightning with its wicked licks—a raspy weather
Fit for trolls and insomniacs.

This storm could push the stars around
Into new constellations
Named for casinos in Vegas.

But it's no dice down here.
I watch the smoke thin from my lips,
Glass of whiskey in a cold sweat.

If you could track happiness
By its spoor and scat, I'd crawl
After every clue, eye on the small signs.

I'd set my traps
In the dark places, in the tangle and stink,
And wait for a sly foot to find one.

Now, over the last gasp of wind,
An old moon drips
Down the pane, erosion of Eros

In the rough light of high summer,
Not like what happens
In a season less insane—

Blossom out of its knot,
Fruit from the puckered bud.
What will it take

For my cadence to come again
To incandescence,
Furious fire along the line?

On the radio, I listen to
That distant hiss between
The hard rock and the warnings,

Until my mind stalls against the static,
And the heart gives up
Its edge, its quick ambitions.

In this lamplit mess,
The clock grinds away, longhand and shorthand
Scribbling the future,

A double-jointed curse
On anything in transit, or anyone
Who hopes to ride it out with the roses.

Sunbreak in the Poconos

The dawn's gone
From pewter to pink, thin streaks
Above the horizon and in the lake
Where ducks ruffle the water
Near the docked rowboats,
Thrust of their noble heads
And the little clown feet paddling below.

How can there be so much world
In one window? Birch and oak
Come clear in the new light, and stones
Stand up in the loose brush
Before the cabin, each morning
A pale return
To the neolithic, perpetual loop
In the long line beyond memory.

I'm watching that rosy glow
The birds fly through, not far from
Branch and berry along the shore.
And miles away, the mountain shows off
Its shaggy hump, where bears
Wake and yawn and go out for breakfast,
Scatter of duff in their backwash.

Tint now of silver in the sky,
But no contrails, no clouds. And no people
On the footpath, the weekend folks

Gone home with their kids and fishing gear,
Back to nasal New Jersey, back
To Ohio of the flat vowels. A cool wind
Stirs the hemlocks and corduroys the lake.
I'll match my breathing to the breeze,
Synchronize my lungs
To the huff and exhalation. Blow, wind, blow,
And move me
As you move the world.

During the Deluge

The rain is having its way with us,
And there's no use nattering at the weather maps
Or calling in experts on the paranormal.

We want the trees fluffy, not all cramped in like this.
The sheen of summer's gone from the muddy gazebo.
It's like living in the spit valve of a big trombone.

All day, the wet abrasions rub us wrong,
And all night, raindrops ricochet from the roof
Like an ogre's lullaby beating us to sleep.

We don't know who to blame, God or Darwin,
And the sky's not taking sides, too busy
Creaming the air down to cold soup.

What does the forecast say? Extra helpings of the same,
And floods backing up in the front yard,
Where the pine tree leans like a swizzle stick.

Oh, let it pour over us like delusions on a beauty queen!
Our hearts are waterproof, and our minds floated off
Three days ago, little rafts on the river of oblivion.

After the Storm, the Birds Begin to Sing

Only an hour ago, the trees were seething,
And now late sunlight breaks in waves

Where the wind arouses them, and me,
Each leaf tip christened with the balm

Of its green name—birch, dogwood, oak—
All of us glistening in the spent rain.

I could root myself in the soaked earth.
I could add my own cracked song,

But silence has more harmony this evening
Under the swish and drip of blown branches.

Though day soon goes down to dark,
This time no part of me goes with it.

It Ain't the Heat, It's the Stupidity

Ah, my city of dog piss and palm trees and vibrating beds!
Around here, moonlight sneaks out like a possum.

I can't stand the grind of going nowhere, cranky
As a pickup truck stuck in the mud.

By the signs for the megamall and the old plantation,
Jesus quotes Himself on every other billboard.

The air's so wet it's like sweet tea leaking
From a widow's dewlap on a cool verandah.

In the Rites of the Wounded Magnolia, they all
Kneel down to the cotton boll and the cannon ball.

Half the people are still in love with the dead,
And everyone I know up north is moving here.

In the Season of Early Dark

1.

The wind sassy and half mad,
The clouds knocked up with rain—
Another feral afternoon in the Midwest,
Fall, and the trees like Salome, ready
To ask, when the last leaf drops,
For my unresisting head.

2.

I'm going to spring all the little traps
Set by silence
And call it mercy. I'm going to let loose
Every thought caught by its hind legs
And screaming for release.
Out of the jaws and sharp teeth,
The tongue comes, loving
The taste of its own blood, gush of words
Hurt into eloquence.

3.

Gray day. Raincoat weather.
Raw wound that would weep over me,
Nasty stuff from so deep inside
It could make the scarecrows gag
Among the stooks and stubble.
Whatever I did to deserve this,
I deserve it.

4.

All the numbers add up—
Mortgages, body count, Lincoln pennies
In a plaster pig my grandfather gave me.
And the years, too, though no one
Knows how many, not the saints,
Not the drugged and corrupt. I have these
Fingers to figure with. They tell me
The end is always at hand.

5.

Misbegotten month
Rushing from bluster to bare bark.
The geese get out of town.
Even the seedy weeds die back,
Brittle slippage of the unloved.
I stack firewood against the stone wall
And plant the last tulips, bone meal
In their shallow holes. Lights rise
From the windows and fall
On the dark grass, so black
My footprints sink down to the roots.

Little Ice Age

October at the edge of cold, the garden coming apart—
Dahlias blunting their soft spikes, a tangle of falling asters,

Leaves giving up the innocence of green, a last flare before
We enter the little ice age where the cricket dies,

Eccentric glitter of ice stiff on the grass blades,
Where breath warms the words to make them visible,

Mother tongue licking the infant sounds into shape.
We're not there yet, still harvesting the gourds

And the hanging grapes, the light still an old gold
Pouring out of the sun, the weeks draining away

Until each day's a death wish, air like a razor,
And nights that beggar everything from bare to barren.

After the Harvest, before the Snow

1.

Shadows lean deeper in the fallen light,
And clouds thicken the air, as if they were
Pools of frogspawn.
I steer myself
By the sticky grid of a spider's web
And its constellation of dead flies.

2.

Should I place a windfall apple on this poem,
A paperweight to keep the words
From blowing away? Schiller
Always wrote on a desktop, with apples
Underneath the lid, inspired by
The rank scent of rotting from within.

3.

Fat for the sparrow, thistle for the finch—
I hang from bare branches
Whatever helps them stay alive,
The little homebodies and the refugees.

4.

Rickrack border of hostas around the house,
Pinwheel dahlias, and the trellis rose—
They've all given up, ghosts
No older than the day they died.

Only the last aster
Stands against the cold, a haggard head
Still struggling to hold on to
Its own penitential crest.

5.

In self-portraits, the artist always
Hides his right hand. And what's up
The sleeve but a paintbrush,
Cruel as a mirror?
In the stubble and squint
Of thin November, I can see
My true face—
The stress and the years and the weariness,
New sorrows of the insoluble.

6.

The jilted trees, sky of sackcloth and soot,
Rain crippling the landscape—
These days I could cry at anything, as though
The leaves were tears for
All of us brought down
By *folie à Dieu,*
The windy madness of man and God.

7.

They say that love
Drives a soft bargain in a hard time.
So, tell me,
In this season of fog and frost,
Leaf-skid and weed-slump, where
Every night's dogged by catastrophe,
Whom do I bribe
To keep the future warm,
Until the coming snows give way again
To redbud and bloodroot
And the wild hyacinth of roadside blue?

Liebestod

All morning, the stubborn roses die by frostbite, around them
The wind like a woman breathing through a hole open in
        her throat.

Season of trapped rabbits, hogs hung low in the slaughter tree.
Season of Hamlet in his skinny tights, blood rankling the brain.

Summer's gone off its medication. You can tell by the way
It stumbled through September, looking a little seedy and
        overripe.

In the next cartoon, a small desert island's stuck on an ice floe,
A man stranded in the lone palm throwing coconuts down at a
        polar bear.

No caption required. No words dark enough to make you laugh.
O Papa Freud, what do you think now about love and death?

I'm for one, against the other. And weren't the roses, red and
        yellow,
Lovely as these leaves in their slow cold float across the sky?

MapQuest to Anyplace Else

I'm afraid of the year before it's even begun, the roads
Paralyzed with ice, the generator coughing sparks.

And where, my love, have you gone? To west Texas,
That colony of barbecue and cow shit? Or Vegas on the freak,

Bad checks and the sick light of sodium poles?
You were never like Kyoto, too beautiful to be bombed.

Always kind to the crazy ones, the failed and lost,
I could wrap my heart in asbestos, fireproof and killing me.

If my days are numbered, let them come
In Roman numerals, like Super Bowls. Out here,

I'm at the sharp end of the argument,
And the wind's still whistling Dixie out of its cold ass.

Gifts out of Dirty Weather

At the mall, three dead weeks before Christmas,
Half the women are old and half are ancient.

All I want under the tree is something to drink,
Bland and warm, and a little butter for my bread.

Up here, in winter where the night ice cracks
Like a knucklebone, some still have this vision:

A windblown paradise of dunes and hula trees,
Salt air and sunburnt rum. But I keep the cold

Close to me. I take it naked into my bed.
Above the fireplace, kings go down on their knees,

Rich gifts laid before the babe, when all he wants
Is his skinny mother, whose only miracle is milk.

Incantations of April

Still winter, and on the local station
Two harvest tunes play out
Their peasant arguments in the dark
Chocolate of a cello, in the keyboard's
Rumble and pluck. So what
If the radio's late, four months
Behind the weather? I'm already
One season ahead, packing up
The corduroy and the watch cap,
The crow's foot jacket in black wool.
Already I'm sniffing the ravaged air
For an odor of new earth, vaguely vaginal,
Compost and loam where the seedlings
Sink their roots. Already I'm turning
Back from stars in their cold glow, and scouting
For sunslicks on the lawn, for the pout of tulips,
Long legs and a painted mouth.
If the trees, bent and bare, look like
A mind naked to its worst woes,
What's that to me? Moon-mad before it's time,
My mission's not to stammer down the streets
Like a salt truck, but to cast a spell
On the calendar, in risky chants, in syllables
Of slow elation, and call up on faith
The random primitives of spring, taking it all
As far as the eye can't see.

Withdrawal Symptoms

I can't speak for the daffodils, but this April snow
Makes my mood blacker than a frostbitten tongue.

For a little sun, I would pray all day and fast till Easter.
But you can't bargain with God—what's in it for Him?

I should move to some hot country, where the people
Live in sand and sandals, and roast whole goats for lunch.

I'll rip from the calendar every picture where winter looks
Soft and adorable, flakes fluffed up in a cozy glow.

What this season needs is some angster rap about rock salt
And the lonely farmer suicides and hand-me-down colds.

It's far too soon for the dog rose and the cattail, but only
A freezing week away from the tall stemware of tulips.

If I can't wait that long, tired of poking the embers
And counting pills in this bitter, self-medicating spring,

I should move to an island of tropical nights, where the moon
Lugs the languid ocean up the beach, one sleepy wave at a time.

Downwind from the Uplift

End of the awkward month, mud
In the birdbath, scum at the curb.
A rat stands on its hind legs and bares
Its great cheese-eating teeth. Welcome home,
Brother: your bed's already made and rank.
Odd how the crocus gulps up, more gold
In its mouth than a Mississippi bluesman.
And only one mean tulip returns, like a fired worker
Come back with a grudge and a shotgun.
A robin struts around the front lawn,
The President of Nothing Much. Neighbor,
Do you feel this season right in the brisket?
Between the plants and the power plant,
Rush hour stalls on the asphalt, fumes and
Thrombosis at the traffic lights. Willows
Let down their dreadlocks; the cherries bloom
With all the inducements of a Dutch whore.
Bystander on the sidewalk, do you think
Nothing bitter will outlast these dark days?
Whatever you see in the gazing globe, or read
In the sparks from a dragtail tailpipe,
We're still at the mercy of men and moon.
Between the dew and the mildew,
The backfall mutinies of rain begin.

Drinking Alone on a Spring Day

AFTER LI PO

New grass grows faster than I
Can cut it,
A punk's twist of green hair
Parted by the wind
And blown so strong the dye bleeds out
From lawn to shadow,
But not over me, raising my glass
To a young world,
And seeing, through that sour mash,
Autumns of my own.
White pear, magnolias in the pink,
Pastels of the tulip—
I sing to them all, a lazy tune
Whose words come back
The long way from my mind,
Early Elvis
Asking for love in the first verse:
Treat me like a fool . . .
And why not? Who isn't a fool
To live past fifty?
Old pine, what can you teach me now?
What song do you sigh
When a breeze from the east
Shakes down
The dead needles in your boughs?
My feet tap out

A dizzy dance step on the flat
Stones of the patio,
The summer chairs already here,
In their laps
The flowers from a fallen drift.
I keep my bottle
Close by, but beyond it
The air's still
Sweet with grief, or else I'm too
Tired to tell
Sorrow from desire, so drunk
I'd like to pour
This whiskey in my open heart,
Beating and beaten,
And feel the bloodrush of heat
Inside these veins,
One more April summoned by the sun,
Before the great
Star chambers of the dark.

May Rain

Evening at morning. Slow drip
In the coffeepot, in the backwaters of the soul.
No picnic in Eden, but cold toast.

In the periodic table, what rare element
Ranks as heavy as this weather,
Blue as the weight of rain?

There's a reason the nervous system
Feels so nervous—dragons prowling the bloodline,
Dottle stopping the pipe.

Faith in remission, I can't pray
Even to those strange saints who have something
A little dark and hairy in the background,

Or call on some minor prophet of the lesser rant
With a nasty line in storms and slaughter,
Whom the ravens refused to feed.

Like ten-gallon oilmen in the West, I want my own
Depletion allowance—I've almost gone
From gush to null.

You could fit my high ambitions under
The shadow of a gnat
And mourn them with a homemade hymn.

What good is spring if it turns
All seethy and irked, forcing the flowers
To a bitter quarantine?

The light here begins in candlewick,
A small urgent flame
Against a sky that pours out its misery.

In this slant rain that warps the window
And smuts the air, nothing
Comes clean,

And no thunder, no groan
To shake the ground and make me tremble
Down to the roots—

Just this crosshatch of cloud
That shades the day from dull to bleak
And keeps the pressure on.

Turn and Return

River, cradle where I crawled into my seedy years,
Bent as the backside of the crescent moon,

You flow wherever you want to, rips and snags and muddy
        grunts,
Overwhelming everything from the squareheads to the
        peckerwoods.

One little sloppy sip of you would make me young again,
Dancing with jukebox women in the third bar of La Casa
        de Los Marinos,

Woozy on Decatur Street, before the Lucky Dogs and the
        drive home,
So late and so drunk the church bells were my lullaby.

There's a black man with a saxophone playing "Stormy
        Weather"
Above your banks, while the sweaty tourists lift their lens

And push the button down, your good side turned to the
        Quarter,
Ferry cutting a scar across you, barges low in the slow curve.

Dirty girl, keeping the gamblers afloat and the chemical
        tycoons,
You spread yourself for me again, always wet and ready,

Spooning against the shoreline as the night slides over you,
The city spent, every reveler looking for his lost room.

II.

Is getting well ever an art,
or art a way to get well?
—ROBERT LOWELL

. . .

The rotting man was first to sing.
—WALLACE STEVENS

Under the Knife

> The whole earth is our hospital.
> —T. S. ELIOT

I dream of his hands
Gloved in blood, my blood,
His fingers counting down
Every knob on my backbone,
And finding there the nerve
That worsens, waiting for
The slip of a late blade.
I'm not too numb to feel
The fear, or a sharp touch
That will cut the future free.
In the dark, under a solar
Zone of lamps, in the cold
And nightmare mess of flesh,
I cannot spare myself,
Even in sleep, or break
The spell that keeps me now
At the mercy of a slow surgeon.

Cuttings from Recovery

Narcissism of the sick,
While the days rot on the calendar.

    • • •

At first, the slender arpeggios of pain.
And then down to
The mule-and-shovel grunts,
Sweaty hammers on the bedrock.

    • • •

I keep repeating the wise advice:
Patience. Nothing too soon.
But if I really knew anything,
Would I still be
Talking to myself like this?

    • • •

The heat and stink of it,
The mysteries dripping in the dark,
The loud rush of drugs before the fade-out . . .

And the party always in another room.

    • • •

When I left here, it was autumn,
The lawns bloated
With body bags of leaves.

Now the snows whir
Around me, like
A beehive of angry plans.

. . .

No music for seven weeks.
Why don't I listen?

Well, why bring music, too,
Into this misery?

. . .

Exile at home, and no one with me
But this woman who warms my blood
Like brandy in the Alps.

. . .

Sleep eases the body back
Into another brave day,
So that it may better feel
The waking pain.

. . .

Outside my window,
Lullaby of the chainsaw,
Inexhaustible north.

Inside the sickroom,
A tired odor seeping from
The wreckage of the bed.

 . . .

Candle grease. Lazarus of one lung. Toy moon.
Among the little enigmas,
Ambition burns away, and words
Rise from the ashes.

Song with One Lung

The wind sprawls in a hurry of snow
Over the graves of tulip and hyacinth.
Six months ago, I dug six inches down
And put them in and turned the light out.
What hope now to bring them back but April?

The cold makes my scars ache. Bleak sun,
Stars hard enough to crack the sky, zero
At noon and in the granite hours after,
Where the weeds blow like scrawny flags.

This season of Euclid and the bare brain,
Even a priest of the sweet impossible
Doesn't have a prayer. All I can see
Are my dead behind me and my death ahead.

Like frozen ink on a frozen page, the pent-up dark
Stays in place, a clot of lampblack and kerosene.
On what feels like the eve of evil, we need
A stock of rock salt to halt the tides of ice
And a new Prometheus to redeem the flame.

Let me crank the furnace and the stereo
To a higher power and wake my veins
With the sting of gin. In this resistant night,
There must be somewhere the first slow push

Of sleepy sap, and I want to be there when it
Rises to the red of rhododendrons, to azaleas
That pink the spring, when my exhausted blood
Will flow again, fresh as the wet light of rain.

Second Slice

Each drug that numbs alerts another nerve to pain.
—ROBERT LOWELL

Infant again
In the long weak days,
An easy collapse
Into someone's hands,
Those knowing, hard-knuckled, hypnotic hands.

. . .

This time, I get it
In the neck, making everything
Hard to swallow.

. . .

Barcode of the winter trees.
And I still can't tell
What all this will
Cost come spring.

. . .

Blood sugar once more
Spiked under the blade.
But why should pain
Sweeten
Whatever's inside me?

. . .

Like a sheriff slow-strolling
To a gunfight, I shuffle the corridors,
Piss bag strapped to my thigh.
Do not forsake me,
O my darlin' . . .

. . .

After the bone spurs and bad discs,
They tightened the spine down
With titanium plate,
Until I was
Shining in my own dark.

. . .

Fog over snow.
Even January ends
Muffled in drugs.

. . .

As before, another high rasp
In the throat, air
Straining into silence, my voice
A tremor
At the vanishing point.

Exit Strategy

Armadas of snow under full sail—
The day finds itself
Lost again in a white horizon,
In the scud and spume of a new year.

I'd like to go against the grain
Of dirty salt and pull the wool blanket
Over my eyes. But I live by the season's decree,
By the laws of North.

If I were a painter, ancient and anonymous,
Master of the School of Endless Winter,
Maybe I could
Soak my brushes in such frozen shades

That even the January winds would
Blow across the canvas
With their sonorous monotonies, like a low
Moaning in a withered lung.

The only color I can see is
A cedar limb with its stole of snow
Where cardinals pick at the cold berries,
Red on red on evergreen.

The world's come down to
Drift and dune, squall and tides,
The sun carried off
By an undertow, the pale polar sky worn away.

More than ever now I miss
The ugly grace of dog-day cicadas,
The stobs in a fall field, gone
With the nappy grasses and broadleaf weeds.

Though I wrapped the roses
In winding-sheets and shook the mothballs
From my cardigan, I left on every shelf
The keepsake dust of summer.

Is it too late to pray
To Our Lady of Perpetual Complaint
And place a taper in the bedroom window
Like a pilot light for the moon?

I wasn't born to hear my own heart
Knock like a steam pipe, or feel my mind
Go numb as a halibut packed under
The business end of ice.

Let this blizzard have its say. I'll turn
The furnace high and wait it out.
In the long argument against winter,
Spring is always on my side.

Residues

Pajama jacket and a crisscrossed robe,
Tartan from some clan of weepy Calvinists,
And nothing underneath
But this tube and the bag I fill
Day and night without trying,
Pale gold from my slow-drip distillery—
Christ, six weeks into the new year
And I'm still
St. Thomas of the side effects,
Resistant to this slippage in the limbs,
The legs gone numb, the right arm that can't even
Raise a fist against its own failed flesh.
And always the hectoring repetition of the pills.

From my sisters, birthday jokes and condolences.
My brother sends an orchid
With a dozen spooky blooms, potted under rocks.
Early evenings, martini lifting the pain meds to a level
Just below euphoria,
I match the music to my mood:
Do I feel tonight like the greasy croon of Faron Young
Or the pinched fiddles of Prokofiev?
Or should I listen to
The constant crackle of cicadas in my inner ear?
How can it be late summer inside
When all around me
The cold quirks of winter have their way?

Here, at the sleepy hinge
Of dream and dawn's rebuke,
My mouth's the only muscle that works at will.
It can pout all morning or repeat
The stubborn lines of old poets. It can lick
The grist and gristle from its lips,
Another meal gnawed down, washed with wine.
It can kiss the mouth that comforts me,
That calms me back
When nerves under fear flare out like lightning.
Sometimes the words stall and hide
Behind the tongue, or cramp up in the mind, or else . . .
—Doctor, deliver this thought with your forceps.

Longtime lackey of tobacco, Luckies now laid aside,
I still crave that drag
And the lungs' release. So, tell me,
What end won't be dark and torturous?
But not yet, not while the moon
Stays up later than I do, enigmas of light
Cloistering the bed. That's why
I bow my neck to this brace and take the medicine—
To let the weak links in the backbone heal.
Shut-in, exit zipped with a scar,
I wait for that day, distant and blue-inched,
When the snows will clear and I'll go out
Only half broken, only one long breath from April's air.

Ceremony

Five months after my divorce from tobacco,
I buy the first pack, tapping
Each one out

And sucking it down to the last reek
And bitter inch, until the air
Blurs to blue.

And soon it all comes back again—
The cough, the sour fingertips,
The charred lungs.

Maybe you can turn away from breathless love,
But not me. I marry my death
With smoke rings.

Not There

Six years ago this month, this May
Where I stall every morning,
Basil still not planted, frail roses
Drying out in pots,

Six years ago I last stepped
Into the crowd on a *vaporetto* and rode
Down the green waters
Away from that ruined lotus of a city
Whose age and injury I feel within myself.

Now William's in Rome with Betty,
Where Michelle and her lover
Stroll their shadows through the ancient streets.
And today, Lynn and Anna-Claire
Will board a plane
For the unspent spring of Paris and Provence.

Oh, Ohio
Has its own art and artichokes,
Its book bins and fountains and chestnut trees
With pale blossoms like pillbox hats.

But I love those lands that touch
The Middle Sea, the south of my longing,
And Spain among them—
Churros dipped in chocolate, blue tiles

Mooring a doorway, the olive groves
That silver in the wind.

Friends, forgive me
For hitching a ride on your lives
Like a flea that fills itself
With any blood traveling past its leap.
My own weak legs
Won't get me far, and my damaged back
Would buckle from the pull of luggage.

When you come home, tell me,
Beyond the cameras and the guidebooks,
How the wine tasted in Cortona
And the moon melted on the waves at Nice.

Toss me a few foreign coins,
As to a crippled beggar
Waiting on the mercy of your return.

Lumbar Complaints

Summer of the sickbed, and all the blowzy flowers
Bloom by neglect, just as Nature intended.

Backbone, you've let me down again, this time so deep
The taproot knocks against the bottom of my blood.

I'm trying to outwit the pain. I'm trying to keep so still
It can't find me, even in the chafing places, in the acid veins.

Hustle of drugs on my dry tongue: they've got me so stopped up
I'll need an enema of warm milk and molasses.

Every sour spoonful, every sly pill makes me feel
Woozy and half mad, like a man harassed by butterflies.

And no lectures, please, no uplift. Let me sleep
In my injured skin, another wasted season gone to seed.

Over and Out

Where do they go, the grasshopper hours? I was reading,
After lunch, the novel of dead children
(Hair in the barbed wire, hats in the wind), and now
Here's the moon, at the end of a sleepy sentence,
Like the bright eye of God on a fallen sparrow.

The mind goes where it wants to—Brazil, the left breast
Of a woman I once knew,
Crocus inching up from the frozen snow. It's like
Shopping at some enormous mall, voluptuous cluster
Of glass and mad money and the runaway heart.

One day, it's biscuits and lullabies; the next,
Assassinations on the satellite dish.
Where did it go, the honeysuckle scent of childhood,
Wisteria hanging its long purple pendants from the pines
And dry husks of cicadas stuck to the bark?

You can call the stones rubies, but will they shine? You can
Take beauty by the throat,
But she still won't kiss you. Sometimes I feel as if
I were born in the bottom of a boot. I would darken my soul
For a joke or a one-way ticket down the wormhole.

I'm turning the clocks back, setting one hand against the other,
And who will stop me?
So what if that's one more mistake, in the cult of ignorance?
I'm like a paralyzed arrow, sap leaking from the smooth wood
And feathers limp, halfway to the nothing behind the nothing.

Indelible Ink

In this time of tattoos, when so many give their bodies
To the mutilating needle, as fashion or manifesto,
And not just a drunken dare gone wrong at midnight,

I feel the word *Pain* tattooed across my spine, in letters
That look the way the German language sounds—
Barbed wire in the jaw, every syllable cranked up to blood.

The poor twist in their hovels, feeding on beans and burnt
      anger.
The wounded-in-war shovel themselves ahead on sticks
      and wheels.
Doesn't the Constitution guarantee us all the right to pain
      and pity?

When I walk, I list to one side, Igor hunched over in heavy
      steps.
It hurts when I lie down. It hurts when I sit. It hurts when
      I stand up.
The nerve goes through my leg like an awl in a plank of
      fresh cedar.

In my neck, in my chest, the spine's held together by a
      small cage
Of crushed cadaver bone and a brace of titanium struts
      and screws.
At the bottom, a swollen knob sends signals of distress to
      the brain.

Here's a pill to make the mind mumble sweet greetings
        to itself.
And here's a pill to open the bowels the other pills have
        blocked.
And the doctors prod and congregate and lay out their
        nasty instruments.

There's ink on my hands and on the page and on the traitor
        backbone,
Too deep for the acids of erasure, for the burr of flesh-eating
        steel.
Dear friends and family, forgive me: I'm waiting to be rescued
        from myself.

Closing In

I know all the ways that things go wrong.
Even an amateur at disaster can see
There's no detour around the rubble, no magic
To sweep the past away like a dog's dirty tail.

It's October of the wet harvest, and already
The dark feels longer than the day,
Cadaverous dark that lies still
Under the late rain, the weeping trees.

Some days, I drift through the afternoon, listening
For rats gnashing their creepy teeth. Some nights,
I dream of gardens in their summer green,
Lilies pulling themselves up by the bootstraps.

I've seen the first birds draft their feathers
For the South, and dead leaves glide over
A windfall of bruised fruit. I play solitaire
With a deck missing the Queen of Hearts.

There's no use trying to repeal the love poems
Because you're frightened by two adjectives in heat
Or by the years that have left you plucking at
The slack and wattles of your own flesh.

If I were fluent in some eccentric tongue, I would
Speak my secrecies in every ear and let them slur
Without crisis or injury, so they would hurt
No one but me, words closing in on a cold end.

Sixty without a Crutch

> I love this world,
> but not for its answers.
>   —MARY OLIVER

In the unnatural science of this age,
Ask my dead mother
Where the laughter went. If I could,
I'd play cocktail piano till the clouds collapsed
Into stars and the stars lined up
As constellations, new ones with names like
Rabbit in a Trap and Hercules Clubbing the Amish,
There, low on the horizon, the spaces between them
Dark and deep as amnesia.

At my age, making sentences while the snow brings in
Its undertaker's chill, I'm prepared to be
Appalled or amused by my elders
In this sorry art, the mad and the randy—
Lowell, that cod of serious weather, blown dizzy
Around the pole; or Lawrence, his lungs like porridge,
Dosing himself with the gray crystals of arsenic,
Poison in the pipes, as if St. Sebastian
Had been put to death by plumbers.

The Age of Heroes has left the building, but left behind
These trashy wars, the pride, the lies,
Smoke drifting from one disaster to another.
I keep telling myself it's not so much

The hate as the humility,
But what can a small joke do
Against the future? I don't think my mind
Has yet reached the late mammalian, still stuck
Among the snaky lobes, neurons in their slither and hiss.

It's been so long since I've felt
The drugged euphoria of August,
Summer now as far away as a foreign country,
Its only ambassador this ash
In the firebox. I suffer the winter
Like withdrawal symptoms. And I remember the wounds,
Remember the day I walked through
The torn field, here and there the snow like bandages,
Soiled strips over the stripped soil.
If I can still sing, at my age, it's no more
Than sepia laments in a minor key.
Every breath in my sandpaper lungs
Comes rasping out like mist on a looking glass,
Ephemera of fog my finger moves through, writing
Lines by which I see myself.
And if the mirror makes a mistake,
Who's to blame? By instinct and error,
I surprise the world until it's gone from wrong to wry.

III.

Where there's no certainty
There should at least be music.
                    —Richard Pevear

• • •

Such joyous remorse, such cranky raptures.
                    —Robert Wrigley

The Blind One

There were three brothers, and one of them was blind.
Ah, his mother said, those dead eyes. Let him see inside
        himself.

And what was that to him? He was always inside himself.
One brother shoed horses, iron ringing in a hot half circle.

The other carried barrels from a ship, all shoulders and rope.
And the blind one? He sang like the night birds, for a penny,

For a dry loaf, for a woman who took him into her own dark.
Tell us what you see, said the strangers, at the end of that
        black stare.

I see the bruise behind my eyelids, and dog piss steaming
        at your feet.
I see the river's stink, water soaked with weeds and heavy
        sweat.

I see the breeze jitter down the streets. Shall I croak the
        raven's song?
It feeds on meat, and I feed on everything I can't forgive
        or see.

Slow Music with Diminished Chords

At the thin end of summer, almost cool,
With a gallant breeze in the treetops,

I and my companions and the wine
Wait for the dark, the flagstone terrace red

Under the last low drenchings of the sun,
As we speak about the excellence in evening air,

In pine and sparrow, all that goes on only as itself
With no grudge against the infinite,

And about the difficult pleasures of the poem,
And the complicated sleep that makes us feel

Obsolete along our own arc, disposable,
A small catastrophe among the mannequins.

At the Casino with Justice

> The perfect ear, the technique, the great gift
> All have come down to this one ghostly phrase.
> —DONALD JUSTICE (1925–2004)

In the cab on Poydras Street, after
    Your play at the poker table,
A tape rolled out

Some Orpheus of the bottleneck
    Testifying to the blues,
I'm a gambler, baby, and then

A high wild run down the frets—
    I can't begin to calculate the odds
Of that tune at that time.

Not your kind of music, but
    Your kind of night—
Good food, good booze, good luck.

In town to honor by our words,
    And his, that late poet
Who was your student, my teacher,

We took a few spring days for ourselves,
    As I led you through
The Quarter and its oyster bars, and down

St. Charles in the green sway of a streetcar,
　　And to Commander's patio, where we ate
A long Creole meal that made you sigh.

I'd kept your poems close even before
　　We met in a California classroom—
Their dry-eyed tenderness of tone,

Their languid, mordant charm, their pang
　　For a South of lost opportunities
Refined in a minor key.

Once, after a lifetime of taming
　　The disposition of syllables
In a thousand cranky lines,

You told a friend how your work
　　Would sift into history:
In the first wave of the second rank.

A man from Miami and its oversalted sea
　　Should know something about waves.
Here, you stepped aboard the Flamingo,

That floating crap game and house of cards
　　Docked all day and dark
At the crook of the Mississippi.

For an hour, I watched you
      Lay down hand after hand,
Folding the risky pockets in seven stud.

Patience and cool and an eye for
      Any edge you could bet—
What did it matter if

The others dropped or raised around you,
      You who might spend years
Nudging a stanza towards the finish line?

And at last you locked into
      A spread that left nothing
To the loose ends of chance.

Turning the down cards over, you heard
      A click of chips
Falling your way, and raked in

The one pot that put you
      Far enough ahead to tip the dealer
And pull up all your stakes.

Girl down on the Farm

Grasshoppers hung up in a high pitch of weeds,
Smear of midges
Riding a low wind across the fields,

And you unruly as a mule with a bur in its bowels,
Looking at every tomato in the patch
Like that red light at the end of a train going anywhere.

Summer again, and no one to court you
In a panama and a seersucker suit, two new wingtips
Stepping over the mudsill,

Only boys in their dusty pickups and tractor caps,
Beer and watermelon at the town picnic,
Flowers fetched up from the wet acres of a graveyard.

You've got more grit than a rooster's gizzard
And spite enough
To burn a schoolhouse down to bitter ash,

So insolent at sixteen that even the dogs
Yelp out of your way like gravel kicked back from a wheel—
You've already had your fill of

Country music and country manners,
Pork fried up in its own fat, and night crawlers
Like convicts at a prison break, betrayed by the moon.

Why does the pines' pure oxygen
Make it so hard to breathe? How can the clear crick
Hold your face that deep in its shallow run?

You'd like to zigzag through the parallels of corn
And knock the edges off
Every foursquare hymn in the family pew, no cure

For Sundays sick of their own slow hours,
When the future feels as distant
As dry thunderheads on an August afternoon.

You've worn out the pages of the catalogue, slicking away
The shoes, the fine-spun dresses, the underthings,
Those slimsy innuendoes of a riper life.

Ain't nothin' out there we ain't got right here,
Your mama says, and you close your eyes,
Practicing amnesia.

In your dark room lit only by
The hot tubes of a radio, you listen to
A world beyond the work boots and plow, a voice

Born on the planet of the saxophones,
Smooth and blue, come down
To lie beside you on the bed, until

You're crazed with ache, the blood
Spurtling through your body like champagne,
Before the static and the ragged silence and the sob.

Boy in the Lull of Midsummer

No fiddles at the picnic that year. Before the stars and
        lightning bugs,
Only a grasshopper at the end of his leap,
A blue jay in the berry bush, his cry like a broken hinge.

Lattice of light through the live oaks, a thin fringe of fingers
Trembling green on the pines, clutching at the wind.
Someone's spilled her Coke again, fresh stains on the
        pinafore.

I've gone quiet as a copperhead, eyes flicking through
        the weeds.
Clink of horseshoes in the shade, and men shouting,
Beer froth and beer bellies, sweat drizzling from the armpits.

Hot as sun with its ravaged hair, the grill wood flares up,
        smoking
Like sinners in the hell pit. It's meat and meat,
While the pickles wilt and mayonnaise spoils in the
        deviled eggs.

I've gone small as a hummingbird, wings beating like a
        frightened heart.
They're singing "Lost Highway" and "Lonesome Me,"
Silvertone guitar with its tinny strings, ten dollars down
        at Sears.

Mothers have lit their cigarettes, wispy mist to keep the
            mosquitoes away.
Have we crossed the border between afternoon and evening,
Or taken the secret detour where time hangs late in summer air?

I've gone shy as a hurt squirrel, hiding behind the high leaves.
Night, take me in, too troubled by myself,
By kin and instinct and litter heaped in the greasy bins.

Patsy Cline on the Jukebox,
Seven and Seven on the Bar

Bitter my tears, and bitter the beer on tap,
Not a Belgian brew among them, just this hopped-up local juice.

My mouth's dry and cracked as a Texas riverbed in deep July,
Lizards stitching their claws all up and down the stony ruts.

I feel too drag-ass low to spin this stool, brain on empty
And face on fire, like a homecoming queen in a combat zone.

Patsy, I've put my buck in that skinny slot. I want to hear you
Fall to pieces, crazy after midnight with the lovesick blues.

Bartender, wipe your wrung-out rag across my eyes and pour
Another slug of that sweet Canadian, this time over ice alone.

My drink's on the rocks, and I am, too. I'm almost ready
For Elvis sweating his heart out on a Vegas stage, fat and done.

I'm almost down on my knees in the sawdust, praying for
Another woman with red hair and three kids and a country croon.

Do the Do

When the drummer tattoos his snare
And puts the hammer down on the high hat,
Taking a stick to the blues,

The band kicks in, Uptown Louie and the Regulators,
Brawl of piano and a foghorn sax, gitstrings
On rhythm and lead, with a fat bass at the bottom.

This ain't no martini music, chanteuse
In a throaty hush, smoke wrapped around her
Like a fox-head stole, brushes soft on the tight skin.

This is mayhem in the neighborhood, rimshots and beer.
It brings the ladies out
Like a hard knuckle knocking at the back door.

It gets the mopes and the gimps and the bedridden up
And slips their sockets loose
Until they do the do with a shaky strut.

Louie's looking good tonight in a Hong Kong suit.
He's got the hair and the sneer
And a voice rough as creosote on a telephone pole.

Skeeter can make his left hand
Slap the scales around until they scream
And leap like the Holy Ghost boogie of Jerry Lee.

That's "Night Train" you hear, Bad Alvin on the honk
               and slur—
Ten years on the road to earn his scars
In a dozen duck-for-cover bands.

It's all jism and jungle, late love and cheroots,
Sweat equity on the dance floor.
Somebody lies about his rusty heart. Somebody don't.

And now it's "Harlem Nocturne," low in the gut,
Time split down the middle
By a midnight clock, air going blue on a slow drip.

Louie nods once at the tired room
And lets the last chord linger, so sweet, so sad
That even the dim light trembles at the end of the song.

Opaque Confessions from the Other Life

> There are
> still songs to be sung on the other side
> of mankind.
>
> —Paul Celan

On the airwaves, the Burundi Quartet is playing
A boyhood adagio by Mendelssohn, that darling little Jew,
Like a slow bee sucking it up from the flower heads.

I'm partial to the banjo myself, that claw-hammer
Clank and spunk, a crowdown over the mulberry tree,
More flare than a hotfoot in the undertaker's shoe.

I've gone beyond the silence of the midnight kiss, the furtive
Touch in a family pew, where half the angels are
Packing heat, with their pimp hats and their mob hyperbole.

Reminder to self: sometimes there's not much distance between
The concert and the concertina wire. Long story short:
No one's marked any shrines on the road map to Babylon.

Though I'm no Moses floating in the wickerwork, I still
Count myself among the orphans, the small fry and the fingerlings.
Chipmunks are cuter than rats, but aren't we all?

The names of the Lord may be infinite, even if
Shithead isn't usually one of them—or, as Borges said,
Sometimes the original is unfaithful to the translation.

Light falls where it wants to fall, not where I need it to fall.
And so does darkness, rippling out like a radio
Dropped in the bathwater, just when I was coming clean.

Swamped

It's been a long time since I was
Anybody's boy on the bayou,
Since I poled a boat around the cypress knees,

Or sucked on a stump of sugar cane,
Or sang wild hymns all night,
Heart beating for Jesus like a tambourine.

I'm never going back. It's too perverse to live
Under a shaky roof, to fetch
Drowsy water from a broken well.

Not every day has to end hung up
In dirty moss, behind it
The moon yellow as a wolf's tooth.

My South goes on without me, a hive built from
The hum and poison of the bees.
The bear has his honey, and I have mine.

Where else, in a land of banjos and fangs,
Where else would I find
This fresh, this inexhaustible rancor and home?

Thanksgiving in New Orleans, 2005

Along the neutral grounds, nothing but dry palms and stunted
    shrubs, all of them rooted in misery, toxic powder on
    the leaves, kicked up when the cars go past, and the
    trucks—the gut-sprung Buick of looters, the Hummers
    crammed with men in camouflage, rattle of guns and
    canteens.

Gray dust rising from this ghost of a city, and outposts of the
    saved afraid to walk out after dark, beyond the failed
    frailty of light. Rush of wind through the avenues like
    the sound of water sucking at the walls.

No scritter of squirrels on the roof. And here and there, no roof.
    Freezers by the curb, tight straps around them, to keep
    in the maggots and the rotted meat. Stuck on the dead
    lawn, on the hydrants, on the bark of live oak, photos
    from the family album, wherever they floated free.

It's too late for another visit from the president, floodlit in
    Jackson Square. The air's clear now of helicopters and
    sailors dangling in the backwash. At the yacht club, an
    orgy of boat upon boat, masts in the portholes, anchor
    up the Evinrude. Pelicans squat on the cracked hulls.

In the Quarter, the girls grind out an extra buck from the
    rescue team, and the cooks at Galatoire's spike a dozen

oysters *en brochette.* Hurricanes slosh down the streets, go-cups sticky and cool, cheap beads noosed around the balconies.

Through the windows of the Garden District, you can see the occasional table laid for a feast, turkey and dirty rice and yams in a casserole, decanters of wine beside the silver candlesticks. And within, you can hear the grace before gravy, dubious prayers that drift on the bone china like spores.

O my city of drowned dreams, even the overflowing lake can't break you. At a club where the levee held, near the bend of the river, someone's stirring a sleepy piano, and not just the black keys, until the night gets up on its tired feet, as it did back in the high times, and does its old, slow, sultry dance.

Outlaw Blues

Tonight's question is: how old should one be to legally think?
Stupidity, too, has its heroes. Ask Bumwipe and Lickspittle,

Lawyers for your third divorce, pawning again the
      family jewels.
You're feeling some better, thank the Lord, but that
      lowdown pain won't quit.

You should be packing your .44 Ventilator, more lethal
      than alimony.
You should be living on dark logic, the unforgettable,
      the unforgiving.

Maybe you need a junky's high, dreamy and sweet,
      a dry wash of brushes
Over the drum skin, taste of bone in the mouth when
      the dope's done.

Under your skull, the *narcocorridos* keep playing, but north
      of the border
You hear those soul records you leaned against at the
      sock hop.

And who's that singing hymns through a bullhorn?
      Mysterious Jesus,
Watch your tongue: Piety's down on its red knees,
      sucking hard

At the rancid appetites, eyes gone sideways in a
      sailor's squint.
That's not your style. You're sleek as midnight, sky like a
      black flag.

But that blowback from the laws of love? It's got you all
      lathered up,
Like a monkey with a grudge and a head full of rum punch.

Church of the Downtown Redeemer
and Twiceborn Saints

Sunday, and the air's gone slack and thick,
Peeled back from the tight night before, until the reverend
Straps it on and knobs it loud, hitting his quick licks
About the Lord, about the going down and the getting up again,
About the slickery pitfalls of body and bottle, and then
He's strangling the live mic like a serpent's head,
Long cord whipping from side to side in the death throes of sin,

Sermon with a backbeat, gutbucket gospel in a neon suit,
And thunder among the pews, lightning in the aisles, a great
Ricochet of amens as he preaches the lid up from darkness
And lets the low souls loose, jitter of black electrics
Through the jacked-up strings and the brazen tambourine,
Crackle of salvation racing down the storm front, making
The pulpit jump and the benches tremble, putting
Mama on the good foot, daddy off the dime,

And the reverend's still kicking it, Fender in full thrash and twang,
Choir behind him at wide-open throttle, angels in fat satin,
So heavy they can lift themselves only by the voice, blessing
The sweat and the spasm and the steam of jubilee,
Reverb pulsing from the amp like waves washing the stain away,
Pools and pools of it, in the rinse of rhythm, the sluice of blues,
A baptism that takes so hard it lasts until the fires of hell
Hiss out and the cinders sizzle and the skin of the damned
Gives off a glow like sweet Easter shining high on
The churchhouse windows, glass in a rapture of risen light.

Bottoming Out

Midsummer and no moon. Low beams on the dry highway.
And that twang from a silver disc? It's Sister Rosetta Tharpe
On her gitbox, raw voice argufying for the Lord.

I no longer know what music suits me. For some moods,
The skeletal airs of oboe and bassoon. And then I give in
To a pigfoot piano, to the bark of a swollen saxophone.

Sometimes beauty becomes so neurotic it can't look at itself.
In the arc of the car, maybe I've taken the last wrong turn,
Gravel under the wheels, gravel under the tongue.

How little we change over the stale years, living
On this small blue stone, not on some planet of tilting rings
In a cauldron of stars. And not even a rumor of moon tonight.

Gauges waver in the radium glow of the dashboard lights.
Beyond the windshield, vapors hang from the vanishing point.
I steer by instinct now, by nudge and muscle and spin.

The mind at midnight travels out on vectors of exhaust,
On its own drone and grind, moving toward some great
            capacious phrase
Fluent as itself, the nomad mind, free among the rude
            mechanicals.

IV.

Muse, teach me the song
That chokes my throat.

—Sophia de Mello Breyner
(trans. Ruth Fainlight)

. . .

Without a woman, with fright,
Plodding on.

—Enrique Lihn
(trans. David Unger)

For Helen, in Her Absence

The house seems so quiet now, now that you're dead.
I almost feel more fear
Than grief, something ancient and naked in the dark.

I still talk to you all day, under my skull
Or in my open voice.
It keeps me close. It keeps me breathing when I want to stop.

I've barely begun to pick through all you left behind—
The white sweater, the emerald ring,
Loose photographs and votive lights in the bottom drawer.

On the square you knitted from the royal colors of Mardi Gras,
Purple, green, and gold,
I place the urn, a solid bronze, heavy even before your ashes.

Where we come from, a thousand hot miles from here,
There's dust of sassafras
Over the gumbo, and in every courtyard a ghost.

I dawdle among the certificates and the sympathy cards.
It's been raining for hours,
And the muddy daffodils lay down their heads in the slop.

So the days go down in cold degrees, and I feel the years
Catching up with themselves,
Shadow after shadow trailing their long desires and remorse.

I take my aching spine upstairs, step by slow step,
To the dead bedroom.
Steady, old man. It's hard now anywhere you fall.

Less than Greek

No Attic tragedy, no daughter slaughtered, or son
Brought to darkness by his own proud hand, in light
Of what he learned, but, on a much humbler level,
Troubles enough, and more than one should bear.

If loss, little or large, pares away until it makes one pure,
What was I then: more human than marble, too dirtied
        with love?
Let me sleep on pillows of burlap, not silk. And let me die
As you did, breathless beside a warm body in my own bed.

Autopsy

For more than a month now, I've been at full flood,
A Mississippi of tears. I think of a thousand ways
To hurt myself, but why bother?

There's already the lawyer and supplemental forms and
Signatures with medallion guarantee, witnesses to
Your cold going and my cold stay.

And here's the urn, a kind of loving cup, capped and disarmed,
No phoenix flaring from the ashes, only a small flame
Perpetual in my mind.

At the funeral home, identifying you before the fire, I saw
A face of inconsolable stone, your hair still silver,
Wet from the undertaker's wash,

Just a few hours after the coroner's table, all those probes
And specimens, abrasions and erasures, fixing
Forever the sliding smile.

I'm making a list of everything that bleeds. I'm asking
The questions no answer can contain. And yet,
What's more stubborn than tomorrow?

Gin and Music

In the living days, in late afternoon, I made
My famous martinis, so dry
A spike of olives would squeak against the gin.

And I would play, at levels even the angels in heaven heard,
Music that suited my mood,
Études or raucous guitar or jazz from the lowlife zone.

But, if you were away on some errand, shopping for
Supper or gadgets in the bargain bin,
I'd keep the house silent, in case you called for me.

These days, when no phone will carry back your voice,
I pause before putting on
Chopin or Hendrix or some smoky diva from the dives.

I take my martinis up, helix of lemon peel in the glass.
And I take your death
Hard: no slow waiting now will bring you home.

To My God, in His Absence

Father, who will rescue me, now that You're missing in action?
Everything I love's gone down to a dark molecular ruin.
Sir, I am afeared, left here with my own wayward urgencies.

I have seen the front-end loader backing up.
I have double-dated Nostalgia and her ugly sister Remorse.
I've been switching tracks like a railroad man in a railroad hat.

These days, even my confusions are doped up on adrenalin.
Somebody must owe me reparations, for I'm feeling mighty
        abused.
Many and many get at the most, and the others creep away.

All those who learned the lessons of gravity from banana peels:
        my people.
All those with little fetuses dancing on their bladders:
        my people.
All those raised in empires of the miserable, with colonies to
        match: my people.

Bless us, Lord, for all our faults and for Your wintry virtues.
I've been standing at the crossroads, supping with a long
        spoon,
Always at the mercy of Your crap shoot and sad astonishments.

The time for miracles is over, for mysteries too bitter to believe.
Sorrow follows me like a dog behind the butcher's truck.
Amen to what I remember. Amen to the sick heart.

Trashing the Shadows

Orphaned again, at an age too late for orphans,
Mother and father long gone under the steel nameplates,
Wife now sifted inside a bronze urn, not that far from
The dowdy flowers of the funeral home, memorial roses
And orchids pink and stiff in their little pots,
Homage of the bloom, homage of the dead petals,
An air of absence settling in the dry soil, circling over me
As I take the wasted plants out with the trash, heavy barrels
Rumbling to the curb on another Thursday afternoon,
Rain washing away the muddy tracks behind them.

Book of the Broken Spine

In my Bible, too, there is no balm in Gilead,
But plenty of spikenard in the jars,
And a sting of poetry on the pages commissioned by King James,
Pages with their half-rankling misbegotten power.

It says there's honey in the hinterland, water in the rock,
But a long way off. I can believe
In distances, in the miles between a dead woman and a miracle.
(And do we meet again in the valley of dry bones?)

I can't put my finger on the fine print, but it must be there,
Maybe among the mad swine
Or the money lenders, maybe spliced in with the spooky angels,
In Eden or Gomorra: no second chance, no quarter given.

On leaves heavy with gold and crimson, the monks put down
Their patient ink, the borders
Crowded with flowers and the gentler beasts. I can still
                almost smell
Smoke curling from the candle stubs, their eyes going
                slowly blind.

For every word that roots itself in the mind, there's another
Called out as wrong, errors teased from

A thorny language, roses blooming crooked in a foreign soil,
Homegrown freaks as beautiful as they are false.

So many enemies fronting the chosen tribes! And so few
Trumpets to bring the ramparts down.
I've followed the story, detours and backwash, from Jehovah
        to Jesus.
And is it all as true as touching the one I love?

When You Hear the Tone

Some go by fire, licked up from hair to bone.
And some go by flood,
That muscle of water wrestling the bodies down.

And you? You closed those tired eyes, slipping into
Dreams too deep to leave—
And the heart tired, too, from loving so much and so many.

Even before, I couldn't bear to imagine all those messy vitals
Hard at work under the skin,
The pumps and sluices, the pulpy bellows sucking it up.

Nor did I like to look at the old clocks, where wheels
And oily hidden springs
Move time ahead of us, always circling out of reach.

Who was it sang, on some scratched record, *I asked for water,*
They gave me gasoline?
I could do close harmony with him on that mean tune.

Or maybe, once more, I should call my own number,
To hear your warm lost voice
Saying its welcome when no one's at home.

I'm down to my last Lucky, with a long night to go.
So baby, please, please, please,
Leave another sweet message on my message machine.

Empty Ever After

Birds still come
To the feeders she once filled,
Spastic little things, jerking their heads
At the insult or in pure confusion,
Some sideways, some upside down,
Wings wrinkling the air until they shake away
To the mercy of a hand kinder than mine.

And underneath the tubes and nylon socks,
At the heaps of spilled seed, I hear
No scratch scratch scratch of rats
With talons and sickening tails.
Even the vermin mourn her
And keep their distance, escaping through
A long raw gouge in the ground.

Missing the Missing

When you were brave and naked and at my side,
What need did I have
For photographs, for any memory so remote from flesh
        and breath?

The rhododendron that once reached our high bedroom
        window
Now fails at its own slow pace,
Half green, half sullen sticks, leaning into the flagstone patio.

I have a picture of you standing before it, that patient smile,
And around your head a halo
Of May blossoms, in some unnamable shade like
        rose-maroon.

But other images take their shape only inside my mind.
You were born to a city
Cradled by lake and long river, daughter of the dew and rain,

Those young summers spent in a cool house your
        grandmother
Kept by the sweaty Gulf,
Afternoons of wet sand, the amniotic bay deep as your knees

Even as far as two hundred muddy yards from shore,
Scavenger gulls in the sea wrack,
Flicker of fish in the small waters around your feet—

O girl I never knew, golden and sunripe, wading back
To the years we lived inland
And up north, safe inside the closed circle of our love!

Dernier Cri

If there's some Abyssinian death cult out there still,
I'd like to join and pay whatever dues they ask, for I am

A griever in bad need of relief. I've put all my marbles on
Going down a black hole after the last breath, atoms of the body

And the smaller particles whooshing into the dark: whither
They go, I go, ashes to ashes, dust to dust, and God help the
        leftovers.

Or maybe there's a new translation that rectifies the old texts,
In which everything I no longer believe is no longer believed,

And there's hope now for even the more debased among us—
Cat ladies and congressmen and those who faint at the sight
        of red meat—

And my beloved waits somewhere on the other side of misery, pale
But always beautiful, knitting a welcome mat for my dead feet.

To the Nth

Blonde as what? Blonde from birth,
And, who knows, before birth, blonde
As sunbreak over the Gulf of Mexico, and goldfall
In the windows of New Orleans when the day's done—

Girl with the golden hair, long crests of curls
Where the light loses itself and finds itself
And shines forever, or until the dark of the body
Presses down and the locks get thinner and shorter,
Each strand clipped into living silver, precious as
Coins placed over the eyes of the warm dead.
As blonde as that, in the memory's nth order of blonde.

Experimental Requiem

You lived through hurricanes and high water, through heat
That would melt the shell from a turtle's bony back,

And through forty-odd years with me. How could you
Sink so low inside the secret currents of sleep?

I may be doing it all wrong. Am I doing it wrong?
There must be some distant funeral rite that sows salt

On the wind until it sounds like whispers on wet glass.
It's a wonder my blood keeps running at this crazy pace.

Hair close cropped, ears with their little lobes, nose
Broken and repaired, and a mouth made for kissing—

O my dead darling, you might as well be here,
No ghost called up by my conjuring, but a presence

That never left, my five wrecked senses set on fire before
The bronze grail that shines around your legacy of ash.

All Too Human

Splinter of lightning in the hot night sky.
It may be the sign of
John the Revelator coming back again, blood dances

On Bayou St. John before it bleeds into the lake.
It may be voodoo I need,
Goofer dust and a chicken foot, tribal rhythms of the body,

Not that God whose kindness has been much discussed
And preached and denied.
You know the one I mean, the old one of the dark testament.

When He's feeling frisky, we get toads and hail, firstborn
Gutted in their cribs.
We get the only son murdered for the greater good.

I've got Akron in my back pocket, New Orleans in my heart.
My mind shines like a new nickel,
And I wouldn't give a dull penny for my thoughts.

On this boulevard of the southern rose, I've seen
Vague haloes around the streetlamps,
My patron saints watching over me in the long rain.

In this season of distress, when the black dog barks,
I'm like a woman who's been
Fucked dry, fore and aft, all her secrets open to the eye.

I remember that other yesterday, waking alone in the
        broken dawn,
Anguish brimming at the tongue.
In the sleepy story of our lives, it's too late for everything.

Late Night with No Wine

You might as well push a .44 hard against my heart
Until the blue steel raises flesh like an extra nipple,
The hammer cocked, the trigger set to a feather's touch,
And then release the lead, a smoky bullet passing through
What's already broken, new hole smaller than the old one.
How many times can you kill a dead man?

I died the day she died, that morning I found her stiff in bed,
The blood pooling low and thick inside her cold body.
How many times can I cry away that sight? Never,
            and every day—
The nerves stripped naked, the mind alive to no man's mercy.

Simple Gifts

Lean against me once more, your hair
Pillowed on my heartbeat. It's been nearly
Nine months since you died: time to be
Born again and fill your lungs with light,
Every new breath an ache and slow release.

This year's late, misshapen Christmas tree
Stands aslant at the window, the strung-out bulbs
Blinking red and green and blue. Soon we'll bring
The family presents down and spread them under
The low boughs of the pine in shaky heaps.

I have no gift for you except this wounded memory.
And what have you brought back for me but yourself?
The gift shops of the dead stay closed forever.
It's midnight, and the fire feeds on old familiar wood.
Lay your head against me, love, and calm my crazy heart.

The Law of Falling Bodies

First the fires of the flesh, and then
A little hammer breaking your harder parts,
Hinge and marrow beaten down to a mealy sift,
So much smaller than the dark resistant stoniness of stone.

Two things I can't live without: water and light.
And make it three: that woman who lay beside me
For more than forty years, blonde gone to gray gone to ash.
In the days of forgetting, the nights last longer than before.

The mind, with its strange affinities, goes back barefoot
Into April, murderous month that suckles its infant kin:
You dead at one end, and at the other a newborn,
First child of our son, sweet Linnea in her cradle.

Galileo leaned out from the leaning tower and let go.
What more proof do I require that we all fall at the
              same speed?
I've given up on blackmail and bribes, the layaway payments
              of prayer.
All I have left is the ropy tenderness of an old man's
              uncertain touch.